D1203151

Freshwater Fish
Piranhas

Launch!
An Imprint of Abdo Zoom
abdopublishing.com

Leo Statts

abdopublishing.com

Published by Abdo Zoom, a division of ABDO, PO Box 398166, Minneapolis, Minnesota 55439.
Copyright © 2019 by Abdo Consulting Group, Inc. International copyrights reserved in all countries.
No part of this book may be reproduced in any form without written permission from the publisher.
Launch!™ is a trademark and logo of Abdo Zoom.

Printed in the United States of America, North Mankato, Minnesota.

052018
092018

 THIS BOOK CONTAINS RECYCLED MATERIALS

Photo Credits: iStock, Shutterstock

Production Contributors: Kenny Abdo, Jennie Forsberg, Grace Hansen, John Hansen

Design Contributors: Dorothy Toth, Neil Klinepier

Library of Congress Control Number: 2017960621

Publisher's Cataloging-in-Publication Data

Names: Statts, Leo, author.

Title: Piranhas / by Leo Statts.

Description: Minneapolis, Minnesota : Abdo Zoom, 2019. | Series: Freshwater fish |
    Includes online resources and index.

Identifiers: ISBN 9781532122903 (lib.bdg.) | ISBN 9781532123887 (ebook) |
    ISBN 9781532124372 (Read-to-me ebook)

Subjects: LCSH: Piranhas--Juvenile literature. | Freshwater fishes--Juvenile literature. |
    Predatory aquatic animals--Juvenile literature. | Predatory animals--Behavior--Juvenile literature.

Classification: DDC 597.48--dc23

Table of Contents

Piranhas

There are many types of piranhas. Piranhas are known for their strong bite. Their jaws are tough. Their teeth are sharp.

Piranhas swim in groups called schools. This helps keep them safe from predators.

Body

A piranha's body is tall and thin. It is covered in scales.

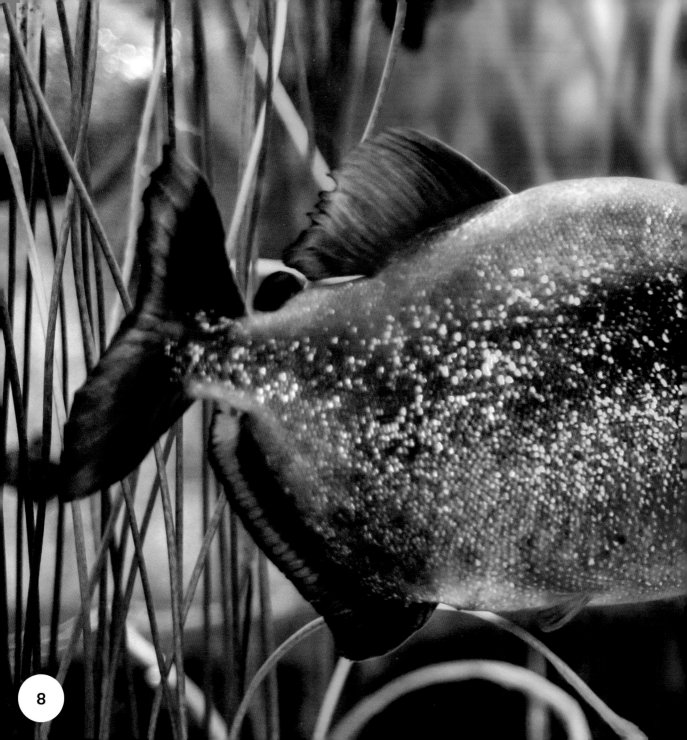

Piranhas have lots of stiff fins. Many have orange or red bellies.

Habitat

Piranhas mainly live in South America.

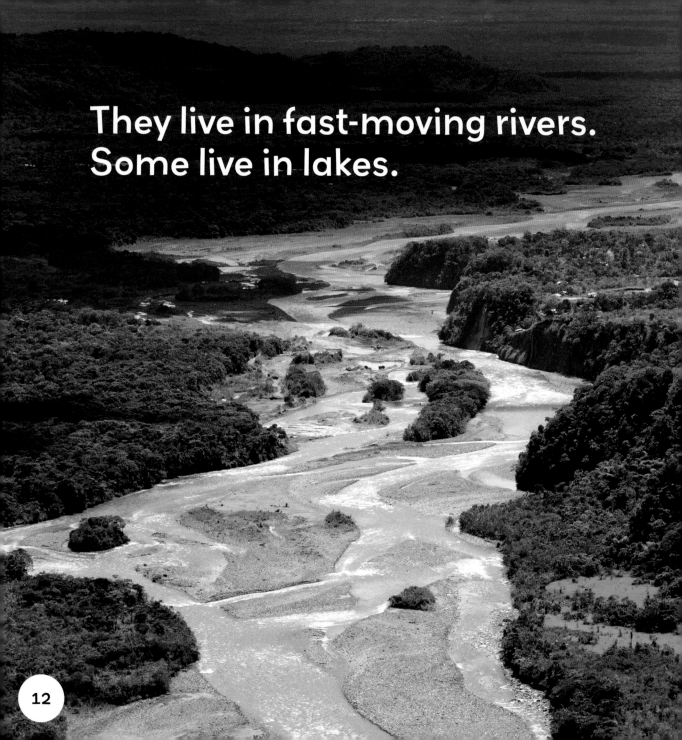

They live in fast-moving rivers.
Some live in lakes.

Sometimes they live in flooded forests.

Food

Piranhas are omnivores.

They eat plants, insects, and other fish.

Piranhas hunt mostly alone. A school of piranhas will work together to attack large prey.

Life Cycle

A female piranha lays up to 5,000 eggs. They hatch after about two days.

Baby piranhas hide in water plants until they are big enough to hunt.

Average Weight

A piranha is lighter than a textbook.

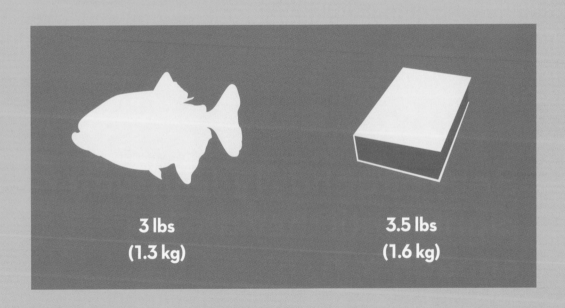

Average Length

A piranha is longer than a basketball.

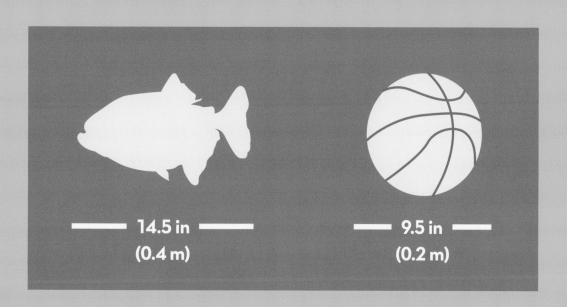

14.5 in
(0.4 m)

9.5 in
(0.2 m)

Glossary

fin – a body part of a water animal that is shaped like a blade or fan.

jaw – the part of an animal's face where its teeth grow.

predator – an animal that hunts others.

prey – an animal hunted or killed by a predator for food.

omnivore – an animal that eats both plants and animals.

scale – one of many small, hard, thin plates that cover a fish.

Online Resources

For more information on piranhas, please visit **abdobooklinks.com**

Learn even more with the Abdo Zoom Animals database. Visit **abdozoom.com** today!

Index